Delegation

Ivan Remus, PE, Esq.

Ivan Remus, PE, Esq.

ALL RIGHTS RESERVED

Delegation © Copyright © 2018 by Ivan Remus, PE, Esq. All Rights Reserved.

All rights reserved. No part of this book may be reproduced in any form or by electronic or mechanical means, including information storage and retrieval systems, without written permission from the author. The only exception is for a reviewer, who can quote short excerpts in a review.

Cover designed by Pro_ebookcovers on Fiverr.com

The examples presented in this book should be considered a work of fiction. The names, characters, places, and incidents, if any, are the product of the author's imagination or are used in a fictitious manner. Any resemblance to real people, alive or dead, events or places is purely coincidental. I am a lawyer, but I am not YOUR lawyer. No part of this book should be construed as legal advice or as any other kind of advice.

Ivan Remus, PE, Esq.

Visit my website at www.IvanRemus.com

You can also visit my professional webpage at www.Ivan-Remus.com

Printed in the United States of America

First Printing: Aug 2018

ISBN-13: 9781790323104

INTRODUCTION

Stop and ask yourself the following questions:

1. Do you have to take work home almost every night?
2. Do you have little time to share with your family, for distractions, or for charities?
3. Do you have a constant accumulation of unfinished work or do you have a hard time meeting the deadlines in your work?
4. Do you spend part of your work time doing things for others, which they could do for themselves?
5. Do you work on the details because you like it, although someone could do it well enough?
6. Do you have a tendency to get personally involved in everything that is happening in your business or company?
7. Do you think you should closely monitor all the details so that someone does their job correctly?
8. Are you frequently interrupted because others come to you with questions or seeking advice or decisions?
9. Do your employees believe that they should not make decisions for themselves about work, but bring you all the problems?
10. Do you spend more time working on details than you spend planning and supervising?

If you answered yes to any of these questions, you need to learn to delegate effectively! So read this book carefully right now, and immediately implement the secrets we reveal here of how to delegate appropriately and effectively. If you follow the steps recommended here, you will notice substantial changes in your professional and personal life.

Now, let me tell you that if you answered in the affirmative to any of the above questions, you are not alone. Very often, managers and employers complain about having a lot to do and having very little time to do all the things they think they have to do. This sensation leads us to have stress and to be inefficient when managing or managing a project or company.

In many cases, managers can reduce stress by practicing one of the most important and poorly understood skills in the business world, which is to delegate.

The inability to delegate has caused the failure of many managers. The information contained in this book is useful to any manager who wants or needs to be more efficient, from company presidents to supervisors, who need to develop the necessary skills for an adequate delegation.

> *"When I assumed the presidency of Bell & Howell I was so busy doing the things that I should have delegated, that I did not have time to manage."*
>
> **Sen. Charles Percy**

Not delegating on time can mean an overload of work for us, creating additional stress that is totally unnecessary.

DELEGATION

Delegate at the last minute induces us to delegate by abdication, which has the potential to generate catastrophic consequences for the company and for us.

Some time ago, one of my mentors asked me a couple of questions that would change the course of my life.

My mentor asked me:

- Do you want to be a millionaire?

My answer was in the affirmative, and he continued telling me:

-If your answer is yes, then why do you insist on keeping to do jobs of $ 10 or less per hour?

At first, I did not understand what he was referring to. I was the kind of executive who loved to be aware and involved in every step of the process. I was proud to know how to do each job within the company. From formatting and running a software program, to filling out a requisition, to balancing a line. Also in my practice as a lawyer, writing a complicated contract, filling out and submitting forms before the different government agencies, balancing accounts receivable and accounts payable. Anyway, I've always liked to learn, and I've never been afraid of work.

He explained that knowing all those things was very good but that doing them was the bad thing. By not wanting to delegate clerical issues, I did not take the time to do what no one else in the company could really do for me. When I tried to do all those things, I was not giving my office the opportunity to grow. I was not giving it the smartest use of my time.

He went further, asking me who did the chores at home. I proudly replied that I was in charge of shopping at the supermarket, doing laundry, washing dishes, picking up at the end of the day. Anyway, all the main tasks of the house were done to perfection as my beautiful mother had taught me when I was a pre-adolescent.

He told me, "Stop doing all those tasks for $ 10 or less an hour." I looked at him with a surprised face. Doing chores around the house is something that has always fascinated me. It not only relaxes me but makes me feel useful to the rest of the family. He replied, hire someone to do it. It is preferable that you dedicate that time to your family or to those projects that have been left at the bottom of the desk drawer for not having time to make them.

That's when he told me something even more profound, **delegate, even when you think you don't have the resources to pay that person for the delegated tasks because doing them is costing you much more than you would have to pay for them**. Time is life. When you say you do not have time for something, what you're really saying is that you have no life.

That same day I began to delegate all those activities that I could delegate. I became a scholar on the subject of delegation. I started asking myself questions like:

Why are there people who seem to delegate without problems and their businesses and their lives are fully developed while it seems that there are other people who, when they delegate something, create chaos and end up being a real nightmare?

What makes a delegation process successful while another apparently similar process ends up being a real disaster?

What things can I delegate that has the potential to create the most significant positive impact by delegating them?

I started to be more jealous of my time. What things are robbing me of my time, are they stealing my life from me? As my mentor wisely said:

> *Time is life. When you say you do not have time for something, what you're really saying is that you have no life*

TABLA DE CONTENIDO

INTRODUCTION	iii
DEFINITION:	1
a. What is "Effective Delegation"?:	4
b. What is NOT "Effective Delegation"?:	5
BENEFITS OF AN EFFECTIVE DELEGATION:	7
a. Benefits for the manager:	7
b. Benefits for the subordinate:	9
c. Benefits for the company:	10
BARRIERS TO EFFECTIVE DELEGATION:	11
a. Possible excuses:	11
b. Possible true reasons:	12
c. The resistance of the subordinate:	13
PSYCHOLOGICAL FACTORS AND HOW TO FACE THEM:	15
HOW TO DELEGATE EFFECTIVELY	19
Effective Delegation Process:	19
a. Adequate planning	20
i. Determine what to delegate:	20
ii. Determine what NOT to delegate:	21
b. Adequate Selection	22
i. Select in whom to delegate:	22
c. Appropriate Assignment	23
i. Of Authority required:	23
ii. Of responsibilities:	24

iii.	Clarify desired results:	24
d.	Adequate Communication	25
e.	Establishment of Time Limit:	26
f.	Adequate monitoring and follow-up:	26
g.	Gratification and Recognition:	28

LEVELS OF AN EFFECTIVE DELEGATION   **29**

DETERMINE YOUR "RETURN OF INVESTMENT" (R.O.I.):   **31**

SUMMARY AND CONCLUSIONS   **34**

   Summary: 34

   a.   Conclusions: 35

EPILOGUE   **37**

CONSULTED BIBLIOGRAPHY: **39**

OTHER BOOKS BY IVAN REMUS, PE, ESQ.   **41**

ABOUT THE AUTHOR   **42**

THANK YOU!   **43**

RESOURCES   **44**

DEFINITION:

The online version of the Oxford Learner's Dictionary defines the verb "to Delegate" as:

"**Delete.** Verb (Del lat. delegāre). [Intransitive, transitive] to give part of your work, power or authority to somebody in a lower position than you.

The before mentioned dictionary establish the origin of the word in the late Middle English: from the Latin delegatus / delegāre 'sent on a commission,' from the verb delegare, from de- 'down' + legare 'depute.'

Resource: Delegate_2 Verb - Definition, Pictures, Pronunciation And ..." Insert Name of Site in Italics. N.p., n.d. Web. 25 Jul. 2018 <https://www.oxfordlearnersdictionaries.com/us/definition/american_english/delega>.

But what does "Power" or "Authority" mean?

Professors Magginson, Mosley and Pietri define "Authority" as the right to send others to act or stop acting to achieve specific objectives. They add that the Authority has two approaches:

- **Formal Authority:** That is given by the same organizational structure of the company.

- **Acceptance of Authority:** Which originates only in those cases when the people on whom the Authority is going to exercise to accept it. Disobedience of a dictated order is the negation of said transmitted Authority. Therefore, it is essential to adequately communicate to all those persons involved in the delegation made.

Leon C. Megginson, Donal C. Mosley and Paul H. Pietri, Jr. Management - Concepts and Applications. The University of Alabama. Harper & Row, Publishers, New York. 1983, p. 249-250.

On the other hand, the same authors express that having the authority that comes with the position is not enough to ensure that the subordinates respond according to the wishes or orders given by the supervisor or manager and clarify that to achieve an "Effective Delegation", it is necessary that the manager or supervisor also exercises his power.

These same authors define "Power" as the ability to influence individuals, groups, decisions or events. In turn, we can identify that there are two types of powers:

- **The Power by Position**: which is derived from the Formal Authority that confers the position that is occupied within the organization chart of the Company.

- **The Personal Power:** which is derived from the followers and depends on how much the followers admire, respect and are committed to their leader.

The Leon C. Megginson, Donal C. Mosley and Paul H. Pietri, Jr. Management - Concepts and Applications. The University of Alabama. Harper & Row, Publishers, New York. 1983, p. 253-254.

From the above we can conclude that the Power and Authority necessary to carry out the delegated task are closely intertwined: You can have the authority that comes with the position or the delegated responsibility, but it is also necessary to exercise the power that is conferred on us by said authority.

As we see, Effective Delegation involves three essential concepts:

- Responsibility,

DELEGATION

- Authority and Power.

- Render accounts or responding for the results obtained.

When the manager delegates, he shares a certain degree of responsibility and authority with the subordinate but is still obliged to account for the result obtained.

In simple words, the generally accepted meaning of the verb "delegate" is obvious: to entrust something to someone; appoint someone his delegate.

The phrase "entrust something to someone" highlights the process of delegation. By delegating, you entrust a subordinate with tasks (along with the authority and power to carry them out), which are part of your responsibility and which, as a rule, you fulfill.

This last point leads us to make a critical distinction between the activities of a subordinate's own position and the assignment that you make of a part of his post.

Figure 1 illustrates the procedure. The example of an executive in charge of a production operation is used. Your subordinate is a production dispatcher.

As can be seen, the executive has assigned the monthly inventory report to his subordinate, the production dispatcher. The subordinate task will be performed by the subordinate one time, the next month the executive will execute it again.

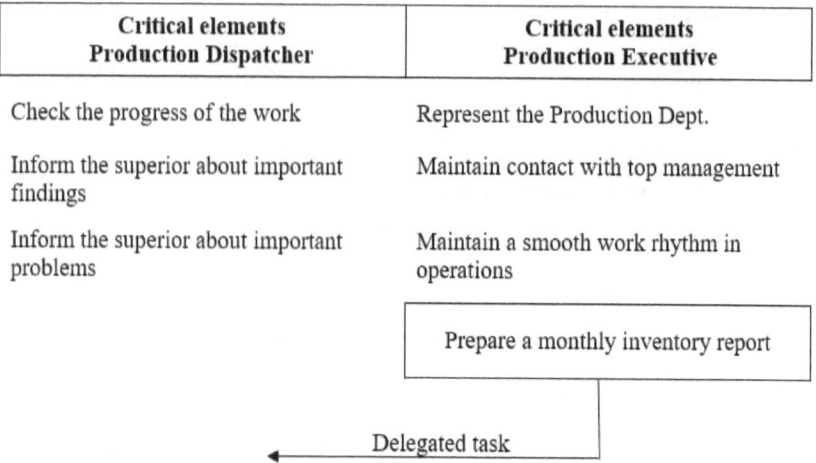

Figure 1: Model of the executive delegation form.

a. What is "Effective Delegation"?:

- Effective delegation is when the manager gives someone part of their responsibility and authority to do something that would typically be part of the work and obligations of that manager and the result obtained is the expected.

- As we have already said, effective delegation involves three essential concepts: responsibility, authority, and accountability or responding to the results obtained. And it is necessary to repeat ad nauseam that when the manager delegates, shares a certain degree of responsibility and authority with the subordinate but is still obliged to account for the result obtained. In other words, delegate the activity but not the result. If at the time of evaluating the results, you are not satisfied with the results obtained, look at yourself in a mirror if you want to find who to claim.

- Effective delegation is usually a procedure to be commonly performed only once. However, an effective delegation could generate that the delegated function is

DELEGATION

transferred permanently, to fit within the description of the subordinate's position.

Particular precaution should be taken concerning this last point: If the company or organization uses formal job descriptions, you should carefully examine them to avoid complications (for example wage claims), to assign the subordinate such task on a permanent basis and the description of their charge does not contemplate its fulfillment. Equal diligence should be taken when reviewing collective agreements that could affect the job description.

b. What is NOT "Effective Delegation"?:

- Effective delegation is not merely assigning a task to a subordinate within its obligations and responsibilities.

- Effective delegation is not abdicating. The manager remains ultimately responsible for the allocation. Therefore, it is essential to establish adequate controls when following up.

- Effective delegation is not to throw undesirable assignments on the subordinate. It should be avoided that the subordinate resents being doing the job of the boss.

- Effective delegation is not to describe in detail how the assistant must carry out the delegated assignment.

For example, you should not delegate reviews of other employees' performance, or the application of disciplinary actions, or the dismissal of an employee. You must create a delegation plan to avoid that it lacks the obvious organizational principles, which would lead to unwanted results.

In our delegation workshop, we teach you the concrete steps you need to follow to achieve adequate, effective delegation and practice with specific and practical examples of how to delegate efficiently and effectively. We also offer specialized consulting services for evaluation and implementation of delegation plans suited to your needs.

> **Reminder: Download the "Delegation Companion Guide" to get your summaries and exercises**
>
> This book has a **Companion Guide** that goes along with it, which you can download for free. It includes critical chapters summaries and implementation checklists. Go here to get your Free Companion Guide and start implementing what you are learning:
>
> **https://ivanremus.com/hbb/delegation-companion-guide/**

BENEFITS OF AN EFFECTIVE DELEGATION:

A real effective delegation generates multiple benefits for both the manager and the subordinate, as well as for the company. Here are some of the benefits of effective delegation:

a. Benefits for the manager:

However effective you are as a manager, the responsibility for your position is higher than what you can assume by your own efforts. Through effective delegation, you can concentrate the most critical issues within the circle of things that you attend and delegate the less important tasks to others. In the above manner, you give the matters of highest importance the attention they deserve.

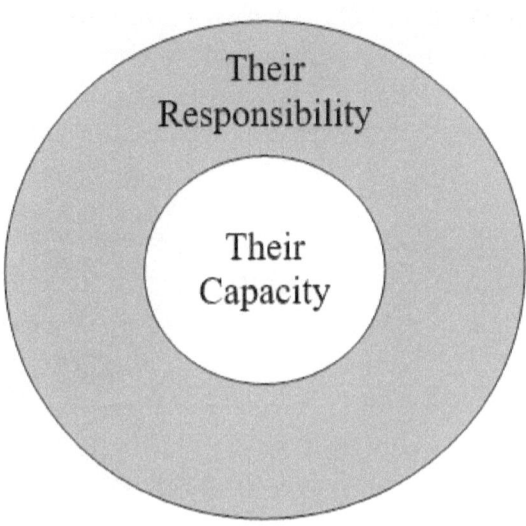

Occasionally, well-intentioned and ambitious managers, but very severely oriented, ignore this reality and try to expand their capacity, hoping that it coincides with their responsibility. It is a task doomed to failure. We often hear managers complain, using phrases like:

- I can not be in five things at once.
- The business collapses if I take a day off.
- I have to do my work and three more.

The results of a Cornell University study allow us to conclude that the manager's positive performance is directly related to the use of effective delegation. In this study, the work practices of a certain number of executives of medium and high rank were analyzed. It was found that among those executives who were judged to be excellent, 75% of them delegated often and effectively, while mediocre executives did not usually delegate at all.

An effective delegation is a valuable tool when it comes to optimal time planning. Next, we present a handy graph to visualize what types of tasks should be delegated, which ones attended at the moment, which ones attended later and which ones simply forgotten.

	Not Urgent	*Urgent*
Not important	**Forget it**	**DELEGATE**
Important	**Plan it**	**Do it now**

Figure # 2: (Eisenhower Planning Matrix)

DELEGATION

Many managers and executives who effectively use the delegation coincide in their opinion that among the positive applications of the same are found:

- It makes your job easier.

- Reduces stress.

- Build trust and empathy with your subordinate.

- It frees you from every day so that you can do what you really should be doing, which is to manage (manage) the company. The more day-to-day tasks you transfer to a subordinate, (with due controls), the more latitude you will have to reformulate the goals of the company or department under your charge, as well as to plan in the medium and long-term, among others.

- Develop your subordinate, so that you can move forward to do more important things. In other words, the more ordinary tasks you transfer to a subordinate, the more latitude you will have to reformulate organizational goals, long-term planning.

- No one expects you, as an executive, to be an expert in everything. Effective delegation allows you to make use of the unique qualities of your subordinate.

b. Benefits for the subordinate:

- It produces opportunities for professional growth.

- Develop their skills.

- It provides personal satisfaction and a sense of achievement and success.

- Expands its value to the organization.

- It gives them the opportunity to evolve with decision-making, which in turn leads to a more significant commitment to the company and the development of a good state of mind and morals.

c. Benefits for the company:

- Save money.

- Increase productivity and efficiency.

- Promotes teamwork.

- Develops a constant flow of new leaders who will be promoted in the organizational structure of the company.

- It encourages "things to go" and prevents chaos from occurring in case of unexpected absence by the executive.

- Generates novel ideas and points of view. A fundamental principle of business is that two heads think better than one. Effective delegation gives you the opportunity to take advantage of the wealth of ideas offered by the intelligence and experience of your subordinate.

- Long-term effects work to the benefit of all parties involved. In general terms, it reinforces the qualities of the executive and keeps him in touch with the elements that are his responsibility, while expanding his horizons, which is beneficial for the company.

DELEGATION

BARRIERS TO EFFECTIVE DELEGATION:

The most significant obstacle to effective delegation is yourself, the manager. When we ask a manager why he does not delegate as much as he should be doing, he gives the following excuses in response:.

a. Possible excuses:

People use many excuses not to delegate as much as they should. Here are a dozen of the most common excuses:

1. I could do it better. I do not like how it looks when someone else does it.
2. I am the only person who knows how to do it.
3. If you want things to be done well, do them yourself.
4. I do not know if I can trust him to do it.
5. No one is qualified or qualified to do so.
6. 6. My people are already saturated with work. I cannot throw more things on their shoulders.
7. You already have too much to do.
8. I do not have the time to teach anyone how to do it.
9. I would be delegating more often if I wasn't so busy.
10. The last time I delegated something to someone, this person broke down, and now I'm not going to give him anything else to do.
11. I do not want to give up that activity because I enjoy doing it.

12. I do not delegate because it costs me money. I do not have enough resources to pay someone else to do that task.

Take a moment to review the excuses you may be offered as reasons for not delegating. Pay particular attention to the last excuse and ask yourself if not delegating those tasks is costing you more money than you would pay someone to do them. Does any other excuse for not delegating come to mind? Be honest with yourself.

b. Possible true reasons:

Behind the excuses that managers raise lies the real reasons why they do not want to delegate. Be honest with yourself to determine what are the real reasons why you do not delegate as much as you should. Among the real possible reasons are:

1. I feel comfortable doing the work I have been doing for a long time. If I delegate such task, I would have to concentrate on new responsibilities, and I do not feel comfortable with it.
2. If someone else can do my job, it could be that they do not need me anymore.
3. **Reverse delegation**. I'm the boss, the boss, I'm supposed to have control of everything.
4. What would happen if the other person "ruins" the thing, I would still be responsible.
5. **Lack of time**. Let's be intellectually sincere: delegating takes time. It is possible that in the early stages of the delegation process you have to invest time in training people. Also, it is also possible that sometimes it takes

more time to complete an activity that has delegated, compared to the time it would take if you do it personally when we also account for the time you have to devote to follow up on the delegate. The important thing is to remember that in the long run that dedicated time is significantly reduced and you will enjoy the fruits of effective delegation.

6. **Perfectionism - fear of failure**. With effective delegation, possible errors are reduced, and the person learns to do the delegated work appropriately.
7. **Shortly staff**. Subordinates who work too much and can not attend to a new load.
8. **Problem with the controls**. This phenomenon occurs in both extremes: Establish too many controls or not establish adequate controls, among which are the following controls.

Take a moment to review the possible reasons you have not to delegate.

c. The resistance of the subordinate:

Sometimes subordinates for various reasons, are reluctant to accept new responsibilities from the boss. Here are some of them:

1. In the past, they have received neither reward nor recognition for a job well done.
2. They may feel it is easier to ask the boss, instead of deciding for themselves.
3. It could happen that they do not have the skill or the necessary skill to do the work.

4. They may feel that they are being forced to do the boss's job.
5. Envy on the part of the other partners of the subordinate's ability.

Study the above list and ask yourself if you have contributed in any way to the resistance of your subordinates. Also, can you think of any other?

**Reminder: Download the
"Delegation Companion Guide"
to get your summaries and exercises**

This book has a **Companion Guide** that goes along with it, which you can download for free. It includes critical chapters summaries and implementation checklists. Go here to get your Free Companion Guide and start implementing what you are learning:

https://ivanremus.com/hbb/delegation-companion-guide/

PSYCHOLOGICAL FACTORS AND HOW TO FACE THEM:

The psychological factor is an essential and critical aspect of the process of effective delegation. The importance is evident when answering the following question: If the delegation offers so many advantages, how is it possible that it is so underutilized? Those who delegate best understand their own mental attitudes and those of the subordinate.

The ideas presented below will help overcome the possible psychological barriers that may arise in the process of effective delegation while assisting them to obtain better results.

- **Be aware of psychological factors**. The field of the mind is subtle and therefore sometimes underestimated. The awareness of the psychological considerations that comprise effective delegation can be of great help for possible barriers that may arise.

- **Address specific doubts**. If you think you are not using effective delegation as often as you should, answer why. Once convinced that you have discovered the obstacle, confront it. For example, if you find out that the specific reason is that you do not have suitably qualified subordinates, you will find in turn that the improved practice of delegation will overcome the problem. The partial delegation and the due training will provide the subordinates of the experience that allows them to accumulate the necessary capacity to face new and more significant challenges in future delegations.

- **Anticipate the attitudes of your subordinates**. The subordinates in whom they delegate are an indispensable part of the psychological considerations that must be taken into account when delegating. Here are some of the reactions potential delegates might show:

    1. **Reward**: If both consider delegation as a reward, their goal of achieving their acceptance and cooperation will be met.

    2. **Boasting**: In some instances, you will run into people who are unsure of themselves and need to get approval from their peers. Possibly this type of person exaggerates the importance that the delegated task really has.

If a delegate suggests to other colleagues that a promotion, an increase in salary or something similar is waiting for you, you should immediately put things in their place and clarify that this is not the case.

    3. **Resistance**: Frequently the subordinate does not like to be entrusted with missions. In general, people in this category have a limited work vision and think that what matters is doing their own work.

This type of employee response is neither constructive nor cooperative. There are two ways left before this type of reaction:

    a. Find another subordinate who is more willing to accept the request.

    b. He takes the time necessary to explain and make him understand that you do not want to take advantage of him or her.

Concrete steps must be taken to achieve active cooperation

DELEGATION

between the parties. One of the most important steps is to realize that there is a better way to interact than the win/lose approach. If the pressure to win can always be removed, the parties are encouraged to cooperate. To do this, we must take into account at all times specific basic rules that are very useful not only for effective delegation but for all types of employment relationships:

1. Respect the world's model of others.

2. The meaning of the communication is the response obtained.

3. The mind and body affect each other.

4. The words we use do not represent the event or the object. The map is not the territory, nor the dinner menu.

5. The most critical information of a person is his behavior.

6. The behavior presented is the best alternative of a person, if he had other options whose behaviors were more appropriate, this (the behavior) would change.

7. The person is NOT their behavior. Do not label people.

8. There are no inept people, only incapacitating states. Everyone has the resources for success.

9. I am in charge of my mind. Therefore I am responsible for my results (achievements).

10. The person with the greatest flexibility of behavior (variety of requirements) controls is the system.

11. There is no such thing as failure, there are only results.

12. There are no tough customers, just inflexible communicators.

13. All procedures must increase resources (alternatives).

Source: "What Is Nlp? - Pci Institute." Insert Name of Site in Italics. N.p., n.d. Web. 25 Jul. 2018 <http://www.pciinstitute.net/nlp/what-is-nlp/>.

Another important psychological factor in the process of effective delegation is:

4. **More excellent knowledge of yourself**: The process of delegation entails the opportunity for a better understanding of oneself. You can determine if you have a feeling of intimate insecurity that is nourished by satisfaction in developing the possibilities of a promising executive, assigning tasks that help him to improve. You test your ability to measure and judge the capabilities of your employees. Effective delegation is a practical exercise.

**Reminder: Download the
"Delegation Companion Guide"
to get your summaries and exercises**

This book has a **Companion Guide** that goes along with it, which you can download for free. It includes critical chapters summaries and implementation checklists. Go here to get your Free Companion Guide and start implementing what you are learning:

https://ivanremus.com/hbb/delegation-companion-guide/

HOW TO DELEGATE EFFECTIVELY

Effective Delegation Process:
Below is a flowchart of the Effective Delegation process:

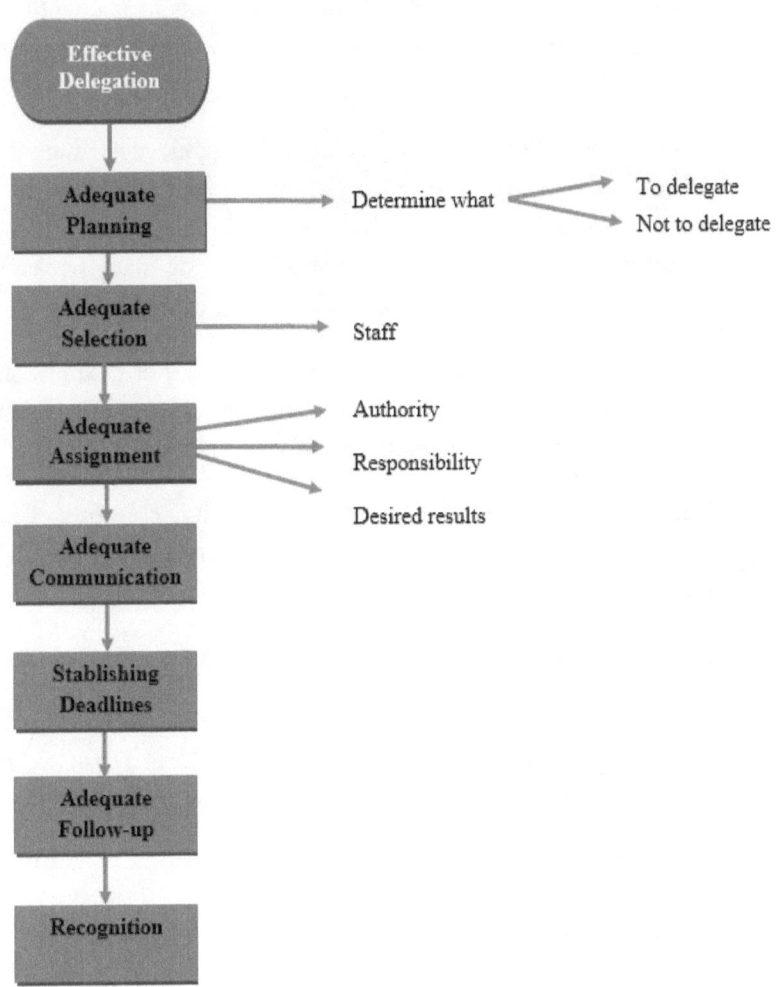

a. Adequate planning

For an Effective Delegation, it is necessary to establish an adequate plan to delegate. As the first step of that plan, we must determine which activities to delegate and which ones not:

i. Determine what to delegate:

When deciding which activities to delegate, we must establish a plan on which events to delegate. We must avoid delegating in a chaotic and disorderly manner. Here are some tips to follow when selecting which activities to delegate:

- Have a clear idea of what you intend to achieve through such delegation. Do you delegate to alleviate your workload, or to provide your assistant with a valuable experience? These objectives are not exclusive, on the contrary, on many occasions, you fulfill different purposes through a single delegation.

- Delegate what is not part of your competence. For example, in a small business, you could delegate the design of your website, business accounting, maintenance of your equipment, etc.

- Delegate routine activities, such as ordering, counting, filling routine reports, etc. You need to focus your time and skills, so get someone else to handle these types of activities.

- Delegate activities or complete situations, instead of isolated tasks simply. (Is not the same:

    * "Send an e-mail to the group advising that we will meet next Friday at eight in the morning. "Versus

    * "Turn on the computer.")

- Delegate the objective or task, NOT the procedure. Of course, this rule has its exception: There are extremely sensitive tasks, which require that they are performed in a particular way and do not admit variations in the procedure of the same. In those cases, then yes.

DELEGATION

- Delegate everything that your subordinate is expected to do in his absence.

- Delegate those tasks that have the potential to develop the subordinate in other competence areas, for their development and potential promotion.

- Always delegate just a little more than you think the person is capable of handling. You will often see how the subordinate does accomplish the appointed task.

ii. Determine what NOT to delegate:

Analyze the time you spend on routine activities, by doing so, determine which ones could be delegated and which ones could be just eliminated. Do not delegate what you can delete. If you should not be doing this activity, perhaps nobody should be doing it.

Among the things that you should NOT delegate we have:

* Performance evaluation of subordinates.
* Dismiss a subordinate.
* Disciplinary matters.
* Confidential issues.
* Planning of long-term business strategies.
* Assignments from our boss that he or she expects us to do personally.

- Be sure not to delegate control of your work team.

- Avoid delegating those tasks that go beyond the subordinate's skills.

- Avoid transferring human relations problems that involve conflicts or difficulties with employees. You should NOT delegate problems that have to do with personal relationships or with the personality of your subordinates.

- Also, avoid delegating emergency tasks when there is no time to train or explain adequately.

b. Adequate Selection

The second step of an Effective Delegation is that of an appropriate Selection of the delegate. In other words, we must determine which is the most appropriate person to delegate the function.

i. Select in whom to delegate:

When deciding which person to delegate the task is the most appropriate, we must take into account that she (he) does not necessarily have the most significant experience or the best skills. Your selection will depend on the time, the place, the nature of the task and the objectives that you want to achieve. Here are some factors to follow when selecting people to delegate:

- **Availability of the subordinate.** The logical thing is to choose that subordinate whose work can be interrupted to carry out the delegated task.

- **Quality vs. Speed.** If speed is essential for you and you have selected a person who usually completes assignments faster than your colleagues, be sure to check the quality of the delegated work, either as you do it or once you have finished. In this way, he makes sure he has not sacrificed quality for the sake of speed.

- **Consider assigning the task to two or more people.** If you wish to assign the responsibility to a person who is not your direct subordinate, it is advisable that you first consult with that person's supervisor. In some cases, it is preferable that this person's supervisor assign the task to you. If you assign the responsibility, do it in the presence of the person's supervisor.

- **Be equitable when delegating.** Distribute the delegations assigned to as many subordinates as possible. Assign a task to a person, but not all the tasks to the same person. In this way, it achieves the training of as many employees as possible and stimulates cooperation among group members while avoiding the appearance of favoritism.

c. **Appropriate Assignment**
- The third step of an Effective Delegation requires an Adequate Assignment of authority, responsibilities, and accountability of the expected results.

Below we will detail each of these concepts to be assigned:

i. Of Authority required:
- The term "Authority" refers to the appropriate power given to the delegate, which includes the right to act and make decisions.
- To paraphrase the definition of the verb "Delegate," we will remember that it was the process in which a first-person transferred to a second person the necessary Authority for the latter to act in the name of the first.

    * "I authorize you to take my vehicle and take it to the workshop to have the oil changed." If I do not authorize you to take my vehicle and you take it (even if it is to take it to change the oil), you would be committing the crime of aggravated appropriation, because you would have taken and would be driving a vehicle for which you were not authorized to drive.

- In this step, the supervisor or manager transfers to the subordinate a limited and sufficient measure of authority within the context of his own position, so that said subordinate performs the delegated task.

    * "I authorize you to take the car to the workshop but not to go for a walk to the next city with the vehicle."

- It is important that we clarify adequately with the subordinate what the limits of said transferred authority are, as well as define the budgetary criteria to be taken into consideration.
- Even if the supervisor grants his delegate the measure of authority

necessary to carry out the delegated task, both should keep in mind that the supervisor is still responsible for carrying out the work and the final results.

- Remember: Be sure to notify anyone who is affected by the transfer of authority.

ii. Of responsibilities:

- The term "Responsibility" refers to the obligation that is created when a subordinate accepts the authority that the superior delegates.

    * "If I asked you to change the oil to the car, complete the task within the time requested."

- It is important to note that managers and supervisors are responsible for what happens or stops occurring in their respective departments. If a subordinate makes a mistake because he has not been adequately trained or because he has been delegated excess responsibilities, you can not blame that subordinate but your manager who exceeded the time to transfer those responsibilities.

- As the executive in charge, you can make the subordinate accountable to you, but the responsibility is still yours and can not be transferred or distributed to your subordinate. In other words, your responsibility does not end when you give instructions, you should verify that such instructions are followed.

iii. Clarify desired results:

- Accountability of the desired results refers to the fact that delegates must respond for their actions and decisions in the execution of the assigned task.

- As we have said, you can make the subordinate accountable to you, but the responsibility is still yours and can not be transferred to your subordinate. In other words, your responsibility does not end when you give instructions, you should verify that such instructions are followed.

DELEGATION

> *   "I asked you to change the oil to the car and have it type W20-50, not cooking oil".

The following chart helps clarify the concepts and how they relate to each other:

You   **Subordinate**

Authority

You can transfer a limited measure of authority within the context of your own position, and only enough to carry out the delegated task.

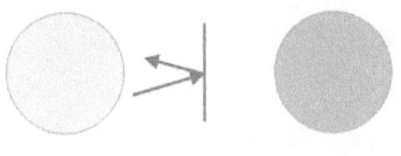

Responsibility

A subordinate can be held responsible within the limits of their own work, but you still have the final responsibility for completing the task.

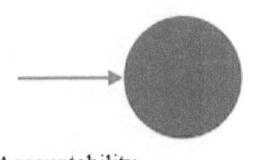

Accountability

You can ask an employee for accounts for their activities and how they perform their employee activities.

d. Adequate Communication

The fourth step of an Effective Delegation requires an Adequate Communication of the authority, responsibilities, and accountability of the expected results, not only to the delegate but to any person who sees or could be affected by the delegated authority.

Remember:

- Be sure to corroborate that the subordinate understands the scope of the task and delegated authority. Be specific Define what decisions and actions you can and can not take and make.

    * If you say, "Do everything you have to do to get it done," it will most likely end up with an unpleasant surprise on your hands if the delegate violates the company's standards.

- Be sure to notify anyone who is affected by the transfer of authority.

e.   Establishment of Time Limit:

The fifth step of an Effective Delegation requires clearly defining how much time the subordinate has to complete the delegated task.

If you want the delegated task to be done within a specific time, make sure that the subordinate knows it and is clear that it must be finished within the prescribed time.

However, it is sometimes possible to negotiate with the subordinate what will be the time required to carry out the delegated task. Make sure that the chosen date is validly accepted by both you and your subordinate. Make sure that both agree, that way you will avoid misunderstandings that cause false expectations.

This aspect is critical. If you tell the subordinate to do the homework when he has time, it is very likely that several days and even weeks will pass before they have even begun to carry out the delegated task.

f.   Adequate monitoring and follow-up:

This step is perhaps the most difficult of all, within the process of an Effective Delegation. It requires establishing control mechanisms that allow it to assess whether the desired goals and objectives are being met, as the delegated tasks are carried out, without falling into the temptation of retaking control and execution of the said appointed task.

Conduct a series of short follow-up meetings, with the purpose of:

DELEGATION

- **Being able to monitor the progress of the delegated task**. Some executives obviate to follow up their subordinates regarding the delegated work, to discover with just days or hours of the deadline that said delegated task has not been carried out and that therefore it will not be possible to fulfill what was promised to a client or higher.

- **Determine the need for assistance from the subordinate**. Some subordinates hesitate to ask questions of their immediate supervisor. They fear that asking will be interpreted as a weakness or lack of capacity for work. Monitoring meetings provide the opportunity to ask what they would otherwise not dare about the delegated task.

The frequency with which you must carry out these follow-up meetings will depend on the complexity of the delegated task and on the experience and capacity of the employee to whom this task has been appointed.

Possibly you will have to hold more frequent meetings with new employees than with employees who have already demonstrated their experience and capacity in tasks similar to the delegated task.

Again we stress the importance of avoiding at all costs the so-called "Delegation to the Reverse" or "Reverse Delegation," which refers to those cases in which the subordinate seeks to return the delegated task to the supervisor.

A delegate might seek to perform poor quality work to avoid being re-delegated to a task. Discourage this attitude firmly by letting the subordinate know that he will have to carry out the delegated task and that he will be evaluated for his performance and performance in carrying it out. Stand firm in your decision and monitor the subordinate closely to confirm that he completes the delegated task accurately. Remember: Be firm in these cases.

Only in extraordinary cases, a manager may have no choice but to return to the delegated task to avoid permanent damage to his performance record.

Whatever the case may be, this should only happen in extreme cases. When you take up a delegated task, the subordinate loses the opportunity to learn and grow professionally, while you recharge yourself.

It is frequent that it is not necessary to return to the delegated task but to give the required support and advice at the appropriate time, through adequate monitoring, hence its vital importance.

g. Gratification and Recognition:

Recognize and reward the subordinate for satisfactorily completing the delegated task.

Allow your subordinates to shine by their own light. Give them credit when they have completed a delegated task. This will make them feel important and satisfied with the work done.

Each person has their particular way of motivating themselves. Be sure to understand how your subordinate feels motivated and create a recognition mechanism around the needs and expectations of his subordinate and not his own.

But be careful: <u>Don't be too generous</u>, because to be so could be counterproductive. Remember: In those cases where the subordinate boasts of the work received in a delegation to his colleagues, it could be misinterpreted that there are favors for that employee.

LEVELS OF AN EFFECTIVE DELEGATION

a. There are four (4) levels of an Effective Delegation, according to the degree of delegated authority:

- **Level 1: <u>Full Delegation</u>**: The subordinate takes full control of the appointed task. Therefore they do not have to consult or participate with the superior.

- **Level 2: <u>Shared Delegation</u>**: The superior and the subordinate agree together who will be responsible for which part (s) of the delegated tasks (s). Extremely useful when the person can perform part of the tasks but is still in the process of learning the rest of the tasks that make up the delegated objective.

- **Level 3: <u>Delegation "You Cover Me in my Absence"</u>**: The subordinate is ready to take charge of the task (s) to maintain the inertia of the business operations when the superior is absent.

- **Level 4: <u>Delegation "Inform me at all times"</u>**: The superior supervises continuously and closely the subordinate, who is not yet ready to take charge of the task alone.

b. In turn, the tasks to be delegated can be divided into four levels, according to their criteria of complexity and importance:

- **Level 1: <u>Insignificant tasks</u>**: Those that DO NOT have to consult or participate with the superior.

- **Level 2: <u>Miscellaneous Tasks</u>**: Those that the subordinate notifies the superior once he resolves them.

- **Level 3: <u>Intermediate tasks</u>**: Those that the subordinate solves after consulting with the superior the solution or possible solutions that the subordinate understands are viable. ("Do not bring me problems, bring me solutions," "Avoid Delegating Upward").

- **Level 4: <u>Vital tasks</u>**: Those that in reality the subordinate has no idea of the possible solutions or the delicate nature of the operation and its potential consequences, requires the superior to supervise and decide the possible solutions before carrying out the delegated task.

The following graphic helps us to understand how the different levels of delegation are interrelated, according to the type of activity to be delegated. The tasks and levels to be delegated are those marked in dark gray. The light gray areas are the ones that are not recommended to delegate.

TASKS / DELEGATION	Insignificant	Miscellaneous	Intermediate	Vitals
Complete				
Absence				
Shared				
Total Supervision				

DELEGATION

DETERMINE YOUR "RETURN OF INVESTMENT" (R.O.I.):

Many entrepreneurs and business owners start their own business because they want to be their own bosses. The problem with the above is that they end up being their own publicists, secretaries, accountants, sales executives, customer service representatives, etc.

Being your own boss means sometimes being your own subordinate and suffer a latent state of work schizophrenia, where we spend unfolded in multiple personalities throughout the day.

Apart from the apparent psychological inconvenience that involves carrying out multiple tasks at the same time, there is the fact that not all the tasks we perform during the day have the same monetary value, especially if we analyze it from the point of view of its return from personal investment or (ROI) for its acronym in English.

Think of all the different tasks related to your work that you do during a week. Determine how much time you spend in each activity, for example, how much time you spend preparing your own stationery or keeping your records, or filing papers, or for example making your own page on the Internet.

Now think about the way you generate your profits. How much do you charge for the services you provide, or how many products could you have sold in that same period?

If you charge an average of thirty dollars an hour ($ 30 / h) and you spend about ten hours (10 hours) filing papers in the week, it means that filing papers cost you potentially three hundred dollars ($ 300.00) in the week. Now extrapolate that amount per month, filing your documents yourself is costing you about 1,200 dollars a month. In short, you cannot continue to afford to submit your papers yourself.

Another way to calculate the cost of daily tasks is to measure it according to the man-hours we dedicate to each task. If we take the last example, devoting about ten hours (10 hours/week) per week was equivalent to forty hours per month (40 hours/month). It means forty hours a month (40 hours/month) that we waste in filing the papers ourselves, instead of dedicating it to share with our family, or resting, or reading a good book, in short, those things in life that we understand that they really are important and are worth doing.

Very often business people come to me and tell me that they are the ones who have made their taxes, or that they have designed their own company logo or designed their website. My question to them is always: Why?

Any person who owns a small business can make their tax return, design their own company logo, or design their website. Any business person could do it, but should they really do it?

The answer to the question in the previous paragraph will depend on how vital the task performed concerning the business is and how much benefit the person obtains from personally performing this task. If you are a designer of Internet pages, then it is essential that you make your own website, but if you are an accountant or a gardener, then not.

In conclusion, we do not need to do everything, and if we try to do everything, some aspect of our business will be affected. We must stay focused on doing what we are supposed to do in our industry.

Many people make the mistake of confusing that running the show is to perform the performance of each of the characters in the full show. However, we are not and should not be confused with the man orchestra.

Managing our business means being able to delegate and understand the fact that others are capable of performing any task as well or better than ourselves. Determining our return on personal investment or (R.O.I) for its acronym in English can help us see what activities related to the business we could or should be delegating and thus free some time to do

DELEGATION

those things more profitable or pleasant.

**Reminder: Download the
"Delegation Companion Guide"
to get your summaries and exercises**

This book has a **Companion Guide** that goes along with it, which you can download for free. It includes critical chapters summaries and implementation checklists. Go here to get your Free Companion Guide and start implementing what you are learning:

https://ivanremus.com/hbb/delegation-companion-guide/

SUMMARY AND CONCLUSIONS

We wanted to present a comprehensive manual that helps the current executive to develop the right skills for an Effective Delegation. We hope we have achieved our goal. Following is a brief summary of the most critical aspects of this manual.

Summary:

- Delegate implies giving or transferring to another person the power or authority to perform some task as if it were ourselves.

- Effective delegation is usually a temporary procedure, often to be done only once.

- Effective delegation is not abdication. The manager remains ultimately responsible for the allocation.

- To achieve active cooperation between the parties, concrete steps must be taken towards a better way of interacting, such as the win/win approach. For this we must take into account, among other things:

    1. Respect the world's model of others.

    2. The words we use do not represent the event or the object. The map is not the territory, nor the dinner menu.

    3. The behavior presented is the best alternative of a person, if he had other options whose behaviors were more appropriate, this (the behavior) would change.

    4. The person is NOT their behavior. Do not label people.

    5. There are no inept people, only incapacitating states.

DELEGATION

Everyone has the resources for success.

6. All procedures must increase resources (alternatives).

- The steps in the process of an Effective Delegation are:

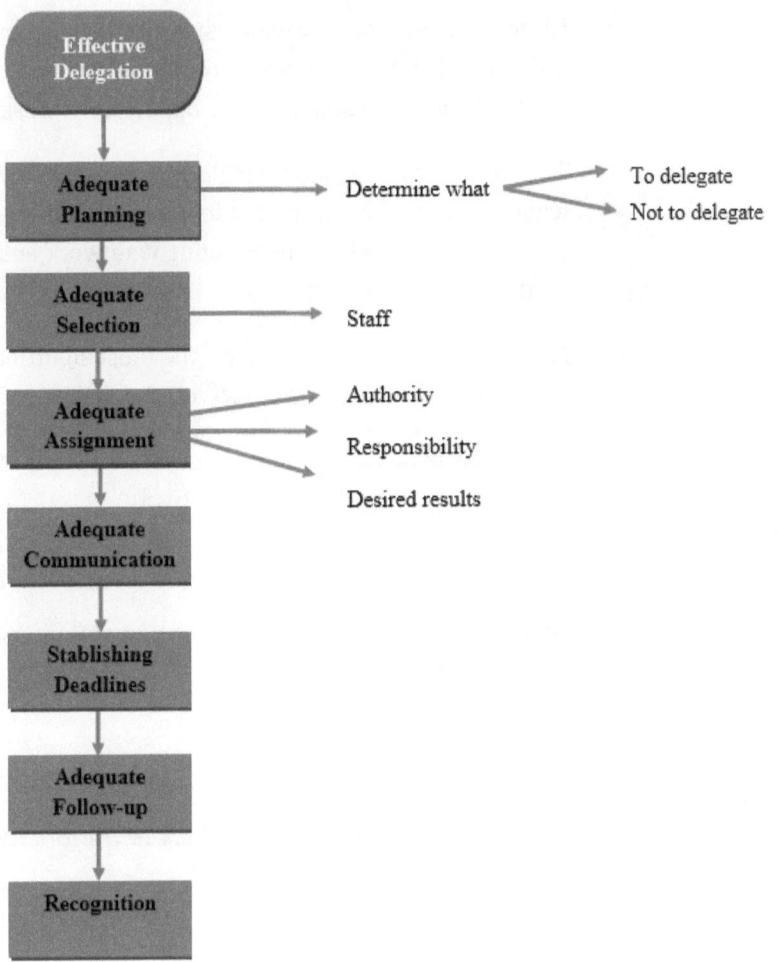

a. Conclusions:

Sometimes subordinates for various reasons, are reluctant to accept new responsibilities from the boss. Here are some of them:

- The Effective Delegation turns out to be an excellent tool for time management because, through the Mass, the manager can concentrate the most critical issues within the circle of things that he (it) takes care of and delegate to the others those less essential tasks.

- Effective Delegation provides opportunities for professional growth and skill development for the subordinate who is willing to take advantage of the opportunity presented.

- The Effective Delegation develops a constant flow of new leaders who will be promoted in the organizational structure of the company, while encouraging teamwork and now money.

- No matter what excuse we give, the most significant barrier to effective delegation is ourselves, the managers.

- It is in our hands to develop the necessary skills to achieve excellence when delegating effectively.

"The decision is yours: You can take the lead and change proactively or remain immobile as the change moves you further and further away from the front."

Gerhard Gschwandtner - Back to the Basics of Selling

EPILOGUE

No matter who we are, we all have the same number of hours per day. Why then it seems that there are people who manage to achieve really extraordinary levels of success, while there is another group of people who appear that the hours of the day are not enough for them, while they do not manage to advance in their professional life and they seem not achieve your economic goals. What makes the big difference? The answer is simple, the first group learned to delegate in a highly effective way while the second group refuses to delegate. In what group do you consider yourself? You do not have to answer me, but I do ask you and answer yourself in which group you prefer to be?

No matter what excuse we give, the most significant barrier to a highly effective delegation is ourselves. It is in our hands to develop the necessary skills to achieve excellence when delegating effectively.

That is why we have wanted to offer you in this book a comprehensive manual that will help you develop these skills. We hope we have reached our goal.

If you want more information, about this or other subjects, you can visit our website www.ivanremus.com where you will find how you can participate in our seminars, training, VIP group and our exclusive personalized consulting service.

Remember that there are only two types of people, those who take the lead to seek improvement and those who choose to remain immobile while the change moves them further and further away from the triumph. In which group do you want to be?

Remember:

Time is life. Every time you say you do not have time for something, what you are really saying is that you do not have life

So, in which group do you want to be?

**Reminder: Download the
"Delegation Companion Guide"
to get your summaries and exercises**

This book has a **Companion Guide** that goes along with it, which you can download for free. It includes critical chapters summaries and implementation checklists. Go here to get your Free Companion Guide and start implementing what you are learning:

https://ivanremus.com/hbb/delegation-companion-guide/

CONSULTED BIBLIOGRAPHY:

- Alec Mackenzie. Gerencia en Acción
  Codado, Caracas, 1972.
- Alexander Hamilton Institute, Inc. La Delegación: El Secreto del Éxito

Modern Business Reports, New York, 1981.

- Leon C. Megginson & others. Management, Concepts & Applications

Harper & Row Publishers, New York, 1983.

- Michael E. Gerber. The E Myth Revisited

Harper Business, New York, 1995.

- Peter Hofstetter. How to Delegate?

AIESEC - National Trainers Team, Switzerland, 1996.

- Karen Lawson. How to Delegate Effectively

Edward Lowe Foundation, New York, 1997.

- Shar McBee. How to Delegate: The 3 L's

Shar McBee, New York, 2001

- Jules Steinberg. How to Delegate

TWICE, New York, 2001.

- E.A. Winning. How to Delegate

E.A. Winning, New York, 2003.

- Methodist Leadership. Management by Delegation

Methodist Leadership, Houston - Texas, 2003

- Tim Bradner. Entrepreneurs Must Learn How to Delegate

Service Corps of Retired Executives, Holland - Michigan, 2003

- Neal Coonerty. How to Delegate & How to Maximize Staff Productivity

Bookshop Santa Cruz, Santa Cruz - California, 2003.

- Gregory P. Smith. How to Delegate Effectively

Chart Your Course International, Atlanta - Georgia, 2003.

- Alan Brown. How to Delegate

Active Information, Better Business, New York, 2006.

- Microsoft® Encarta® 2006. © 1993-2005 Microsoft Corporation.

OTHER BOOKS BY IVAN REMUS, PE, ESQ.

The lawyer Ivan Remus has several books to his repertoire within the theme of Management and Leadership, among which are:

Negotiation.

Delegation.

Letters from a Divorced Father - The Other Side of the Moon.

Likewise, a series of books on the vital topic of Self-Help and Motivation is currently being developed.

The complete list can be found at www.ivanremus.com

It is also important to note that all your books are available in both English and Spanish languages.

ABOUT THE AUTHOR

Ivan Remus is a renowned lawyer and engineer who holds the Master Practitioner designation in Neuro-linguistic Programming (NLP) and has admitted to practice law in at least ten federal courts, including the Supreme Court of the United States (SCOTUS).

His successful career in the legal, engineering, real estate, and academic fields is extensive and focuses on business consulting. Mr. Remus, who has personally pledged to contribute to the practice of law through his private practice and academic legacy, has enjoyed a reputation as a passionate and dedicated executive, with extensive experience and proven success in complicated negotiation processes.

He is also the author of numerous books in the fields of business administration and leadership, as well as in the area of self-help. You can follow him on his blog: www.IvanRemus.com

THANK YOU!

Ivan thank you for buying and reading this book. I hope you find it an interesting and useful guide on how to achieve success when negotiating every aspect of your professional and personal life.

Before leaving, would it be okay with you if I ask you a small favor? Could you take a moment and leave a brief comment of one or two lines on the website where you bought this book? Your review can help others decide what to read next. I would be greatly appreciated by many other readers.

**Reminder: Download the
"Delegation Companion Guide"
to get your summaries and exercises**

This book has a **Companion Guide** that goes along with it, which you can download for free. It includes critical chapters summaries and implementation checklists. Go here to get your Free Companion Guide and start implementing what you are learning:

https://ivanremus.com/hbb/delegation-companion-guide/

RESOURCES

If you want additional information, on how you can participate in our seminars, training, VIP group and our exclusive personalized consulting service, you can visit our website. Let me know if you are interested in me coming to your city to give a talk or training on this or any other topic.

www.ivanremus.com

**Reminder: Download the
"Delegation Companion Guide"
to get your summaries and exercises**

This book has a **Companion Guide** that goes along with it, which you can download for free. It includes critical chapters summaries and implementation checklists. Go here to get your Free Companion Guide and start implementing what you are learning:

https://ivanremus.com/hbb/delegation-companion-guide/

www.ingramcontent.com/pod-product-compliance
Lightning Source LLC
Chambersburg PA
CBHW030532220526
45463CB00007B/2798